Until the story of the hunt is told by the lion, the tale of the hunt will always glorify the hunter.

– African Proverb

ISBN: 978-0-9979635-7-1
©2019 Delina Pryce McPhaull. All Rights Reserved.
Published by E&P Books.

For additional resources, visit wokehomeschooling.com

OH FREEDOM!
Journal

**For Reflection, Creative Expression
and Conscious Learning**

This journal belongs to:

_____

HOW TO
Use this Journal

This journal was designed to be used as you go through "Oh Freedom!" history lessons in your homeschool. As your parent/teacher reads, as you listen to the audiobooks and watch the videos, take some time to take notes on what you're learning. It's possible that you don't have a lot of practice taking notes yet, so this journal will guide you through that.

The Headlines. Write a summary of all that you learned in your history lessons that week. What stories interested you most? Which ones would you like to tell a friend? If you have trouble thinking of these, imagine that you're a online newspaper or cable news reporter. What information would people need to know about the most? **From all the things you learned in history that week, pick the top 4.**

Put a pin in it. There is so much more to learn. Most of the time, we're just skimming the surface. **List the people, places or events you would like to learn more about.** These are just reminders for a later time.

New words. You'll be hearing a lot of new words. Sometimes you'll have to stop your parent/teacher and ask, *"What does that mean?"* **Write the word down so you won't forget.**

Reflection. The goal is to do more than just take in information. Think about what you're learning in history and how it connects to today. **Take at least seven (7) minutes to reflect on what you've learned. There are several ways you can do this:**

- Journal some of the answers to the questions in the *Oh Freedom!* curriculum.

- Write about how the information made you feel.

- Pretend you are in another time period. Write through another's perspective.

- Write more about one of your headlines. Why was that story interesting to you?

Make sure you are in a quiet space for these 7 minutes of reflection. Do whatever helps you focus – soft music, essential oils, deep breaths, etc. Don't worry about getting the dates right or spelling the words right. **Just think and write.**

ACTS of God. In every situation, in every point in history, you can see God at work. Take some time to talk to God. Express adoration — why do you **"Adore"** (love) God? **Confess** – sometimes you know in your mind and heart the right thing to do and you don't do it, or you do the opposite. Confess those big things and little things to God. **Thank** God for everything in your life — your family, your brain capacity, your friends, your home, the opportunity to learn at home and everything else you can think of (trees, clean air, etc.). Finally, S stands for **Supplication**. This is where you ask God for the desires of your heart. Ask for God to supply for the needs and desires of others.

The last page is a blank canvas for you to create. Use it to be creative — write poetry, doodle, do hand lettering, etc.

We are excited that you are using this journal and learning more about U.S. History. Most of all, we hope that as you reflect on what you're learning, you will be inspired to create a better tomorrow for everyone.

TOPIC:

DATES:

This week, I learned:

Pretend you're a reporter deciding on the most important things to share from this week's history lessons.

1.

2.

3.

4.

I want to learn more about:

▶

▶

▶

▶

▶

▶

New Words:

My Reflections

Prayer Box

A

C

T

S

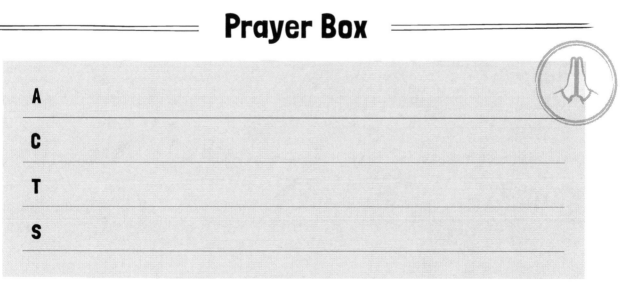

TOPIC:

DATES:

This week, I learned:
Pretend you're a reporter deciding on the most important things to share from this week's history lessons.

1.

2.

3.

4.

I want to learn more about:

▶

▶

▶

▶

▶

▶

New Words:

My Reflections

_____

_____

_____

_____

_____

_____

_____

_____

_____

_____

_____

_____

_____

Prayer Box

A _____

C _____

T _____

S _____

TOPIC: [_____]   DATES: [_____]

This week, I learned:

Pretend you're a reporter deciding on the most important things to share from this week's history lessons.

1.

_____
_____
_____
_____
_____
_____

2.

_____
_____
_____
_____
_____
_____

3.

_____
_____
_____
_____
_____
_____

4.

_____
_____
_____
_____
_____
_____

I want to learn more about:

▶
▶
▶
▶
▶
▶

New Words:

My Reflections

Prayer Box

A

C

T

S

TOPIC:

DATES:

This week, I learned:

Pretend you're a reporter deciding on the most important things to share from this week's history lessons.

1.

2.

3.

4.

I want to learn more about:

▶

▶

▶

▶

▶

▶

New Words:

My Reflections

Prayer Box

A

C

T

S

TOPIC: DATES:

This week, I learned:

Pretend you're a reporter deciding on the most important things to share from this week's history lessons.

1.	**2.**	**3.**	**4.**

I want to learn more about:

▶

▶

▶

▶

▶

▶

New Words:

My Reflections

Prayer Box

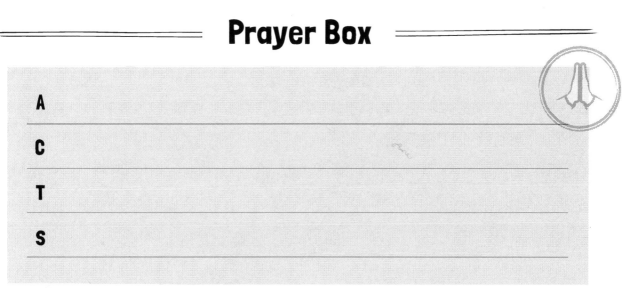

A

C

T

S

TOPIC:

DATES:

This week, I learned:

Pretend you're a reporter deciding on the most important things to share from this week's history lessons.

1.

_____
_____
_____
_____
_____
_____
_____

2.

_____
_____
_____
_____
_____
_____
_____

3.

_____
_____
_____
_____
_____
_____
_____

4.

_____
_____
_____
_____
_____
_____
_____

I want to learn more about:

▶

▶

▶

▶

▶

▶

New Words:

My Reflections

Prayer Box

A

C

T

S

TOPIC:

DATES:

This week, I learned:

Pretend you're a reporter deciding on the most important things to share from this week's history lessons.

1.

2.

3.

4.

I want to learn more about:

▶

▶

▶

▶

▶

▶

New Words:

My Reflections

Prayer Box

A

C

T

S

TOPIC:

DATES:

This week, I learned:

Pretend you're a reporter deciding on the most important things to share from this week's history lessons.

1.

2.

3.

4.

I want to learn more about:

▶

▶

▶

▶

▶

▶

New Words:

My Reflections

Prayer Box

A

C

T

S

TOPIC: ⬚⬚⬚⬚⬚⬚⬚⬚⬚⬚ DATES: ⬚⬚⬚⬚

This week, I learned:

Pretend you're a reporter deciding on the most important things to share from this week's history lessons.

1.	2.	3.	4.
_____	_____	_____	_____
_____	_____	_____	_____
_____	_____	_____	_____
_____	_____	_____	_____
_____	_____	_____	_____
_____	_____	_____	_____
_____	_____	_____	_____

I want to learn more about:

▶

▶

▶

▶

▶

▶

New Words:

My Reflections

Prayer Box

A

C

T

S

TOPIC:

DATES:

This week, I learned:

Pretend you're a reporter deciding on the most important things to share from this week's history lessons.

1.

2.

3.

4.

I want to learn more about:

▶

▶

▶

▶

▶

▶

New Words:

My Reflections

Prayer Box

A

C

T

S

TOPIC:

DATES:

This week, I learned:

Pretend you're a reporter deciding on the most important things to share from this week's history lessons.

1.	2.	3.	4.
_____	_____	_____	_____
_____	_____	_____	_____
_____	_____	_____	_____
_____	_____	_____	_____
_____	_____	_____	_____
_____	_____	_____	_____

I want to learn more about:

▶

▶

▶

▶

▶

▶

New Words:

My Reflections

Prayer Box

A

C

T

S

TOPIC: DATES:

This week, I learned:

Pretend you're a reporter deciding on the most important things to share from this week's history lessons.

1.

2.

3.

4.

I want to learn more about:

▶

▶

▶

▶

▶

▶

New Words:

My Reflections

Prayer Box

A

C

T

S

TOPIC:

DATES:

This week, I learned:

Pretend you're a reporter deciding on the most important things to share from this week's history lessons.

1.

2.

3.

4.

I want to learn more about:

▶

▶

▶

▶

▶

▶

New Words:

My Reflections

Prayer Box

A

C

T

S

TOPIC:

DATES:

This week, I learned:
Pretend you're a reporter deciding on the most important things to share from this week's history lessons.

1.

_____
_____
_____
_____
_____
_____
_____

2.

_____
_____
_____
_____
_____
_____
_____

3.

_____
_____
_____
_____
_____
_____
_____

4.

_____
_____
_____
_____
_____
_____
_____

I want to learn more about:

▶

▶

▶

▶

▶

▶

New Words:

My Reflections

Prayer Box

A

C

T

S

TOPIC:

DATES:

This week, I learned:

Pretend you're a reporter deciding on the most important things to share from this week's history lessons.

1.

2.

3.

4.

I want to learn more about:

▶

▶

▶

▶

▶

▶

New Words:

My Reflections

Prayer Box

A

C

T

S

TOPIC: DATES:

This week, I learned:

Pretend you're a reporter deciding on the most important things to share from this week's history lessons.

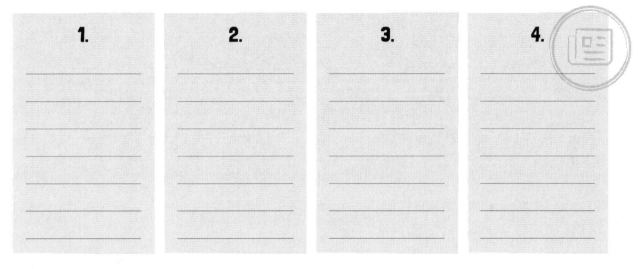

1.

2.

3.

4.

I want to learn more about:

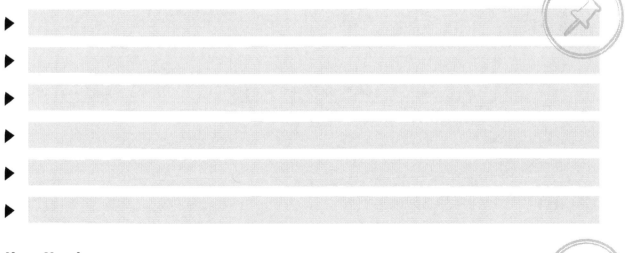

▶

▶

▶

▶

▶

▶

New Words:

My Reflections

Prayer Box

A

C

T

S

TOPIC:

DATES:

This week, I learned:

Pretend you're a reporter deciding on the most important things to share from this week's history lessons.

1.

2.

3.

4.

I want to learn more about:

▶

▶

▶

▶

▶

▶

New Words:

My Reflections

Prayer Box

A

C

T

S

TOPIC: ⬜   DATES: ⬜

This week, I learned:
Pretend you're a reporter deciding on the most important things to share from this week's history lessons.

1.	**2.**	**3.**	**4.**
_____	_____	_____	_____
_____	_____	_____	_____
_____	_____	_____	_____
_____	_____	_____	_____
_____	_____	_____	_____
_____	_____	_____	_____

I want to learn more about:

▶

▶

▶

▶

▶

▶

New Words:

My Reflections

Prayer Box

A

C

T

S

TOPIC: ⬚⬚⬚⬚⬚⬚⬚⬚⬚⬚⬚⬚ DATES: ⬚⬚⬚⬚

This week, I learned:

Pretend you're a reporter deciding on the most important things to share from this week's history lessons.

1.

_____
_____
_____
_____
_____
_____

2.

_____
_____
_____
_____
_____
_____

3.

_____
_____
_____
_____
_____
_____

4.

_____
_____
_____
_____
_____
_____

I want to learn more about:

▶
▶
▶
▶
▶
▶

New Words:

My Reflections

Prayer Box

A

C

T

S

TOPIC:

DATES:

This week, I learned:

Pretend you're a reporter deciding on the most important things to share from this week's history lessons.

1.

2.

3.

4.

I want to learn more about:

▶

▶

▶

▶

▶

▶

New Words:

My Reflections

Prayer Box

A

C

T

S

TOPIC:

DATES:

This week, I learned:

Pretend you're a reporter deciding on the most important things to share from this week's history lessons.

1.	2.	3.	4.

I want to learn more about:

▶

▶

▶

▶

▶

▶

New Words:

My Reflections

Prayer Box

A

C

T

S

TOPIC:

DATES:

This week, I learned:

Pretend you're a reporter deciding on the most important things to share from this week's history lessons.

1.

2.

3.

4.

I want to learn more about:

▶

▶

▶

▶

▶

▶

New Words:

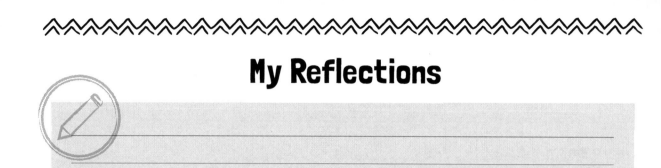

My Reflections

Prayer Box

A

C

T

S

TOPIC: DATES:

This week, I learned:

Pretend you're a reporter deciding on the most important things to share from this week's history lessons.

1.

2.

3.

4.

I want to learn more about:

▶

▶

▶

▶

▶

▶

New Words:

My Reflections

Prayer Box

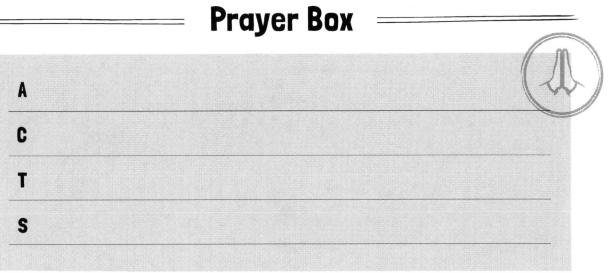

A

C

T

S

TOPIC:　　　　　　　　　　　　　DATES:

This week, I learned:

Pretend you're a reporter deciding on the most important things to share from this week's history lessons.

1.

2.

3.

4.

I want to learn more about:

▶

▶

▶

▶

▶

▶

New Words:

My Reflections

Prayer Box

A

C

T

S

TOPIC: ⬚ DATES: ⬚

This week, I learned:
Pretend you're a reporter deciding on the most important things to share from this week's history lessons.

1.	**2.**	**3.**	**4.**
_____	_____	_____	_____
_____	_____	_____	_____
_____	_____	_____	_____
_____	_____	_____	_____
_____	_____	_____	_____
_____	_____	_____	_____

I want to learn more about:

▶

▶

▶

▶

▶

▶

New Words:

My Reflections

Prayer Box

A

C

T

S

TOPIC: [   ]   DATES: [   ]

This week, I learned:

Pretend you're a reporter deciding on the most important things to share from this week's history lessons.

1.	2.	3.	4.
_____	_____	_____	_____
_____	_____	_____	_____
_____	_____	_____	_____
_____	_____	_____	_____
_____	_____	_____	_____
_____	_____	_____	_____
_____	_____	_____	_____

I want to learn more about:

▶ _____

▶ _____

▶ _____

▶ _____

▶ _____

▶ _____

New Words:

My Reflections

_____
_____
_____
_____
_____
_____
_____
_____
_____
_____
_____
_____
_____
_____
_____

Prayer Box

A _____

C _____

T _____

S _____

TOPIC:

DATES:

This week, I learned:

Pretend you're a reporter deciding on the most important things to share from this week's history lessons.

1.

2.

3.

4.

I want to learn more about:

▶

▶

▶

▶

▶

▶

New Words:

My Reflections

Prayer Box

A

C

T

S

TOPIC: DATES:

This week, I learned:

Pretend you're a reporter deciding on the most important things to share from this week's history lessons.

1.

2.

3.

4.

I want to learn more about:

▶

▶

▶

▶

▶

▶

New Words:

My Reflections

Prayer Box

A

C

T

S

TOPIC: [   ]   DATES: [   ]

This week, I learned:

Pretend you're a reporter deciding on the most important things to share from this week's history lessons.

1.

_____
_____
_____
_____
_____
_____

2.

_____
_____
_____
_____
_____
_____

3.

_____
_____
_____
_____
_____
_____

4.

_____
_____
_____
_____
_____
_____

I want to learn more about:

▶

▶

▶

▶

▶

▶

New Words:

My Reflections

Prayer Box

A

C

T

S

TOPIC: _____ DATES: _____

This week, I learned:
Pretend you're a reporter deciding on the most important things to share from this week's history lessons.

1.
_____
_____
_____
_____
_____
_____

2.
_____
_____
_____
_____
_____
_____

3.
_____
_____
_____
_____
_____
_____

4.
_____
_____
_____
_____
_____
_____

I want to learn more about:

▶ _____

▶ _____

▶ _____

▶ _____

▶ _____

▶ _____

New Words:

My Reflections

Prayer Box

A

C

T

S

TOPIC:

DATES:

This week, I learned:

Pretend you're a reporter deciding on the most important things to share from this week's history lessons.

1.

_____
_____
_____
_____
_____
_____

2.

_____
_____
_____
_____
_____
_____

3.

_____
_____
_____
_____
_____
_____

4.

_____
_____
_____
_____
_____
_____

I want to learn more about:

▶

▶

▶

▶

▶

▶

New Words:

My Reflections

Prayer Box

A

C

T

S

TOPIC:

DATES:

This week, I learned:

Pretend you're a reporter deciding on the most important things to share from this week's history lessons.

1.

2.

3.

4.

I want to learn more about:

▶

▶

▶

▶

▶

▶

New Words:

My Reflections

Prayer Box

A

C

T

S

TOPIC: ⬚⬚⬚⬚⬚⬚⬚⬚⬚⬚⬚ DATES: ⬚⬚⬚⬚

This week, I learned:

Pretend you're a reporter deciding on the most important things to share from this week's history lessons.

1.	**2.**	**3.**	**4.**
_____	_____	_____	_____
_____	_____	_____	_____
_____	_____	_____	_____
_____	_____	_____	_____
_____	_____	_____	_____
_____	_____	_____	_____

I want to learn more about:

▶

▶

▶

▶

▶

▶

New Words:

My Reflections

Prayer Box

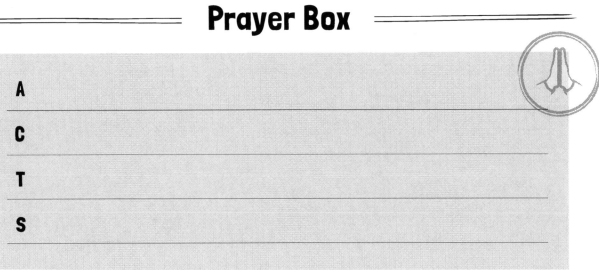

A

C

T

S

TOPIC: DATES:

This week, I learned:

Pretend you're a reporter deciding on the most important things to share from this week's history lessons.

1.

2.

3.

4.

I want to learn more about:

▶

▶

▶

▶

▶

▶

New Words:

My Reflections

Prayer Box

A

C

T

S

TOPIC:

DATES:

This week, I learned:

Pretend you're a reporter deciding on the most important things to share from this week's history lessons.

1.

2.

3.

4.

I want to learn more about:

▶

▶

▶

▶

▶

▶

New Words:

My Reflections

Prayer Box

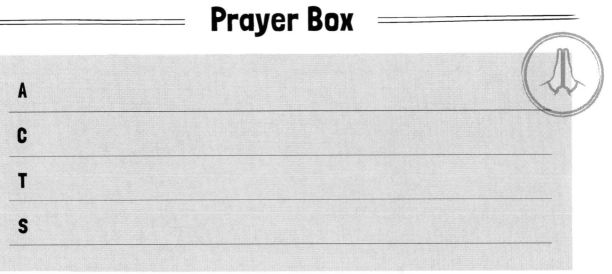

A

C

T

S

TOPIC:

DATES:

This week, I learned:

Pretend you're a reporter deciding on the most important things to share from this week's history lessons.

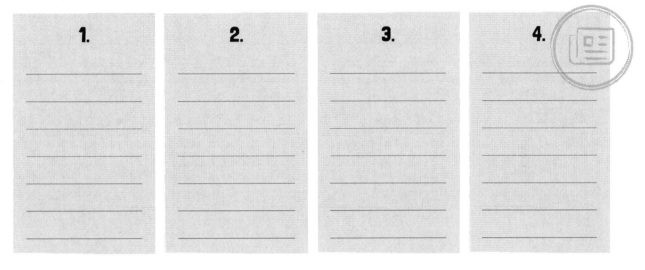

1.

_____
_____
_____
_____
_____
_____
_____

2.

_____
_____
_____
_____
_____
_____
_____

3.

_____
_____
_____
_____
_____
_____
_____

4.

_____
_____
_____
_____
_____
_____
_____

I want to learn more about:

▶

▶

▶

▶

▶

▶

New Words:

My Reflections

Prayer Box

A

C

T

S

TOPIC: 　　　　　　　　　　DATES: 　　　

This week, I learned:

Pretend you're a reporter deciding on the most important things to share from this week's history lessons.

1.

2.

3.

4.

I want to learn more about:

▶

▶

▶

▶

▶

▶

New Words:

My Reflections

Prayer Box

A

C

T

S

TOPIC:

DATES:

This week, I learned:

Pretend you're a reporter deciding on the most important things to share from this week's history lessons.

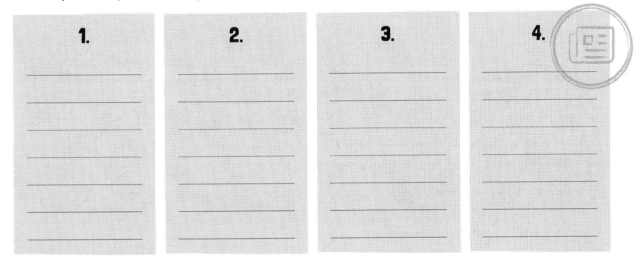

1.

2.

3.

4.

I want to learn more about:

▶

▶

▶

▶

▶

▶

New Words:

My Reflections

Prayer Box

A

C

T

S

Made in the USA
Middletown, DE
23 August 2020